# The Orange Shirt Story

Author: Phyllis Webstad

Illustrations: Brock Nicol

When Phyllis was a little girl, she lived with her Granny on the Dog Creek Reserve, part of the Stswecem'c Xgat'tem First Nation. Their home had no electricity and no indoor toilet. In the summer, when the sun was hot, Phyllis would cool herself off in the bathtub full of water that Granny kept in her garden.

Phyllis and Granny lived off the food they grew in Granny's garden and berries from the land. Granny and Phyllis would go to the Fraser River and catch fish. They would eat some fish for dinner and dry the rest on the drying rack to save for winter. They didn't have much, but they got by with what they had.

Growing up, Phyllis felt lonely. There weren't many children on the reserve to play with.
Each September, all the older children, like her cousin, would leave the reserve to go to school.
Phyllis looked forward to the day that she could go too.

Phyllis didn't get many hugs when she was little. But she did have Granny, and Granny's house was a safe place for everyone on the reserve. There were lots of people who came to Granny for help and advice. Phyllis's favourite place to be was Granny's kitchen.

When Phyllis turned six in July, Granny made her a cake to celebrate her birthday.
Granny told Phyllis, now that she was six, she was old enough to go to school. When September came,
she would go to the residential school, St. Joseph's Mission, for the first time.

Phyllis was excited about going to school so she could play with her cousin and the other children.
She wanted to find out what happened there and hoped she would make some friends.

Before her first day at school, Granny took Phyllis into town to buy her a new shirt.
They didn't have a car or a truck, so when they went into town,
they would take a blue bus that they called 'the stage'.

Going to town was exciting! They took the stage down a noisy and bumpy dirt road. Soon the bumps stopped and the noise hushed. Phyllis looked out the window and saw a paved road whizzing by underneath them.

The town was so loud and busy, with people and vehicles everywhere!
There were shops to visit and restaurants to eat in. One shop had a red and white pole outside of it.
Phyllis watched it twirl round and round and she wondered where the stripes were going to.

Granny took Phyllis to a restaurant, and they sat at a booth with a mini jukebox.
When Phyllis dropped a coin into the slot, the box would play a song for her. Phyllis ordered breakfast with two eggs.
When they came, they were sunny side up. It was like they were looking up at her from the plate!
Phyllis didn't know how to eat them — Granny's eggs were always scrambled.

After breakfast, Granny took Phyllis to a shop that was filled with clothes and toys.
Phyllis picked out a shiny orange shirt that laced down the front. It was bright and exciting!
She felt as excited about the shirt as she did to go to school.

Granny bought the shirt and they got back on the stage and went home.
Phyllis held the bag with her orange shirt in it all the way.
She promised herself that she wouldn't wear it until the big day when she went to school.

Phyllis waited and waited and, finally, the day arrived. Phyllis, wearing her shiny orange shirt for the first time, said goodbye to Granny. Granny patted her on the head and said, "what loves it." Phyllis got on the stage with all the other children and waved at Granny from the window.

It was a two-hour journey to get to the residential school — much further than Phyllis had ever travelled before. She stared out of the window, waiting to see the place where they were going.

When they arrived, Phyllis started to feel very scared.
The residential school was so much taller than anything she had seen before.
The building seemed cold and unfriendly, as unfriendly as
the nuns who came out of the school to meet them.

Phyllis asked her cousin how long they had to stay there.
Her cousin said that it would be 300 sleeps before they could go home. 300 sleeps?
That sounded like forever!

The nuns took all the children inside and walked them down a long hallway in single file.
In a room, the children were undressed and made to take a shower.
Phyllis had never seen water coming out of the walls before!
Phyllis didn't want to take off her shiny orange shirt, but the nuns made her.

After she had showered, they gave her different clothes to wear. She didn't like them.
The nuns put Phyllis in a chair and cut her hair short. She asked for her orange shirt back,
but they told her that she wouldn't be allowed to wear it anymore.
Phyllis cried, "Give it back. It's not yours, it's mine. My granny bought it for me!" but no one would listen.

The residential school wasn't where Phyllis learned. It was the place where the children slept and ate. Phyllis soon realized that the nuns didn't care if she was tired, sick, hungry, or sad. She had to rely on herself. It felt as though she didn't matter. At dinnertime, Phyllis and the other children would eat tasteless and almost colourless food.

There were pale-green, moon-shaped beans that tasted awful, and there was smelly fish that definitely wasn't like the salmon that she and Granny used to eat together.

At night, Phyllis wondered why Granny was not coming to get her. She would cry herself to sleep. In her dreams, she would play in Granny's garden and go salmon fishing in the river.

Each day, the children went into town to attend public school. Before boarding the bus, they picked up a small carton of orange juice and brown paper bags with their lunches inside.
Some days one or two children got a chocolate bar in their lunch.
Everyone would look to see if they had one too, but their lunch bags just had sandwiches in them.

It felt like the grown-ups were playing a cruel joke on them.
Phyllis took the bus to public school with her cousin. Every day the bus driver dropped
her cousin off at a different school. Phyllis wished she could go with her.
She didn't understand why they couldn't be together.

At school, Phyllis learned to read and write with all the other boys and girls, but she was still lonely. All the children from the residential school were lonely because they had been taken away from their homes and their families.

Her teacher was a curly-haired redhead. She was as nice as she smelled. She would smile at Phyllis and help her with her lessons. Phyllis wished she could go home with her teacher at the end of the day — she made being at school bearable.

Phyllis liked her teacher, but she was no substitute for Granny.
She wondered what Granny was doing while Phyllis went to school every day.
Phyllis missed her home and the garden.

She started counting the days until she could go back again.
Each day the number got smaller and smaller.
She waited and she waited.

The other children at school could order books from a book club, but none of the residential school children were allowed to get any. Phyllis didn't understand why they were treated differently. She wanted a book, too. Why wasn't she allowed one?

In the playground, she was just like all the other boys and girls.
At lunchtime, everyone played together. Phyllis learned to swing on the swings
and would wrap her swing around the pole and watch it unwind.

The best time of day was when the bus came to pick them up after school. Phyllis always saved a seat for her cousin. When it came to her stop, her cousin would run on the bus and plop down next to Phyllis. Sometimes she would bring onions that she picked on the school grounds.

Her cousin would say, "Waaannt some?" and Phyllis would laugh at her onion breath.
But Phyllis was always so hungry! She would grab an onion and eat it like an apple.
Her breath smelled just as bad as her cousin's did.

On the bus, they learned to sing songs together.
They sang, "We are the missions, mighty, mighty missions. Everywhere we go, oh, people want to know, oh...
who we are... so we tell them, we are the missions…"

The seasons changed from fall to winter, then to spring and finally, it was summer again. Phyllis was excited about going home. She never wanted to go back to the residential school, or see the cold-hearted nuns ever again.

After 300 sleeps, the stage came and took Phyllis back home to the reserve.
She was so happy to be back to a place where she mattered, a place where people cared about her.
That summer, she stayed at home with her Granny.
She stayed in her familiar house and worked with Granny in the garden.

She went fishing for salmon in the Fraser River, and she ate them for dinner.
She had everything she needed, and she never went back to the residential school again.
Not every child was as lucky as Phyllis.
~ The End

**September 30th  Orange Shirt Day:**
Today the residential schools have closed for good.
She and her family learn about and celebrate their culture.  Phyllis knows what it means to be
Northern Secwépemc, and she is proud of who she is and who her people are.

Each year, on September 30th, many people including Phyllis wear bright orange shirts
to honour residential school survivors and their families. Orange Shirt Day kicks off
talks about anti racism and bullying at the beginning of the school year.

Phyllis's true story is only one among many. We must listen to these stories, and we must learn
from our past. By doing so, we can walk into the future without making the same mistakes again.
When we wear our orange shirts on Orange Shirt Day, we reaffirm that every child matters —
the children from every nation around the world, the residential school survivors,
and the First Nations children who didn't come home.

About the Author:

Phyllis Webstad (nee Jack) is Northern Secwépemc (Shuswap) from the Stswecem'c Xgat'tem First Nation (Canoe Creek Indian Band). She comes from mixed Secwépemc and Irish/French heritage. She was born in Dog Creek and lives in Williams Lake, BC. Phyllis is married, has a son, a stepson, three grandsons and one granddaughter.

Every year, Phyllis and her family camp by the Fraser River near Williams Lake. The old and the young come together to catch and dry fish just like their ancestors did. These are lessons that Phyllis learned as a child. Now, she is proud to teach her grandchildren the ways of her people. Phyllis is a third-generation residential school survivor.

She earned diplomas in Business Administration from the Nicola Valley Institute of Technology and in Accounting from Thompson Rivers University. Phyllis received the 2017 TRU Distinguished Alumni Community Impact Award for her unprecedented impact on local, provincial, national and international communities through the sharing of her orange shirt story.

**Glossary:**

• Residential school: A boarding school maintained by the Canadian government for First Nations children from sparsely populated settlements.

• Public school: A school funded by the Canadian government where all children can go to learn and grow.

• Reserve: A piece of land set aside by the Canadian government as a place for First Nations people to live.

• Drying rack: A rack made of wood where fresh salmon hung to dry so that it could be eaten in the winter. They would light a fire with green tree branches under rack so the smoke would keep the flies away.


**Conversation Starters:**

• What do you think it might have been like to attend residential school?

• Have you ever spent a long time away from home? What did it feel like?

• Can you imagine being away from home for 300 sleeps?

• What did Phyllis do to find happiness?

• What do you do when you're feeling sad or lonely?

• Why do we wear orange shirts on September 30th?

BELLA
COOLA

WILLIAMS
LAKE

GRANNY'S
HOME

DOG CREEK
RESERVE

ST. JOSEPH
RESIDENTIAL SCHOOL

LAC
LA HACHE

Map of Phyllis Webstad's Story!

(Not to scale)

VANCOUVER

# A Story of the Secwépemc (Shuswap) People

For more than 8,000 years, the Secwépemc (Shuswap) people and their ancestors have lived along the Fraser, Thompson, and Columbia rivers of present British Columbia. Ancient stories say the people were present on the earth as it formed.

The land was made suitable for the Secwépemc by Senkéwelc (Old One or Creator) who made many new plants and animals, shaped the land, and led the people into the territories they would occupy. He gave them the languages they would speak and also told them to respect all their relations, not only people but also plants and animals. Senkéwelc sent Transformers into the territory, the most powerful of whom was Skelép or Senxwéxwlecw (Old Coyote). The Transformers made the earth a better place for people and taught them how to prosper. Many ancient Secwépemc stories are told about how the land was made, where the ancestors lived and died, where the best foods and medicines were found and how the territory had been defended. Stories connect Secwépemc people to their land.

Twenty-nine Secwépemc bands, each with several villages and a government, prospered in Secwepemcúl'ecw, the land of the Secwépemc, which extended from the Rocky Mountains in the east to beyond Setetkwa (Fraser River) in the west. Trade routes linked the Secwépemc people to other First Nations, including people beyond the mountains. People of other nations were allowed to enter Secwepemcúl'ecw only with permission or if they had Secwépemc family.

The Secwépemc used all parts of their territory like a ranch, traveling widely in appropriate seasons to known productive sites where they gathered food, medicine, and materials. All resources of the land were shared with other Secwépemc people - sharing was a principal duty. Elders, parents and children worked together to manage their land with fire and other techniques to increase production of foods and medicines. They also developed sophisticated skills for collecting, preserving and preparing foods. The people prospered.

Families were the most important basis of Secwépemc society. Children learned by working alongside adults and by respectful guidance from parents and elders. Ceremonies and traditional stories taught the children their history and the importance of respecting their traditions and values. When children came of age, they acquired a guardian spirit to give them strength for their role in life. Education of children gave them a sense of self-confidence, empowerment, responsibility and pride in their culture.

The Secwépemc welcomed the first white people, the fur traders, to their land and helped them to survive. Secwépemc people and fur traders worked well together with mutual respect. But then more immigrants came with European diseases, especially smallpox and measles which were previously unknown to the Secwépemc. About two-thirds of the Northern Secwépemc people died of the diseases. Entire Secwépemc villages, once large and bustling, were now burial grounds which held only memories of living people.

Only seventeen villages remained.

The Cariboo gold rush brought many more immigrants. Miners and settlers took the Secwépemc land and waters with little respect for Secwépemc rights or traditions. The Secwépemc were confined to tiny parcels of land called reserves and told they had no right to the vast territory they once controlled. No treaties or other mutual agreements were made. The people lost their land while the new government imposed racist laws which influenced nearly every aspect of Secwépemc life, including the education of children. The Secwépemc people have advocated strongly for their rights from the beginning and, in recent years, they are being increasingly supported by Canadian society. The Secwépemc people remain strong.

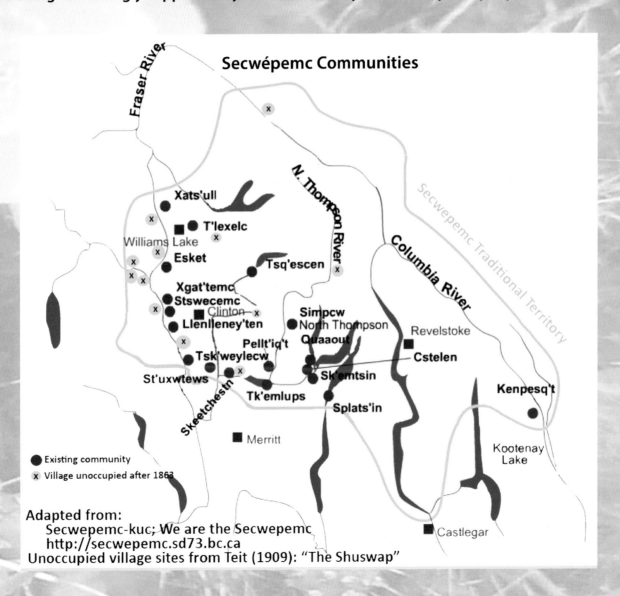

## Secwépemc Communities

Fraser River

N. Thompson River

Columbia River

Secwepemc Traditional Territory

Xats'ull

T'lexelc

Williams Lake

Esket

Tsq'escen

Xgat'temc

Stswecemc

Clinton

Simpcw
North Thompson

Quaaout

Revelstoke

Llenlleney'ten

Cstelen

Pellt'iq't

Tsk'weylecw

St'uxwtews

Sk'emtsin

Kenpesq't

Skeetchestn

Tk'emlups

Splats'in

Kootenay
Lake

Merritt

● Existing community

x Village unoccupied after 1863

Adapted from:
   Secwepemc-kuc; We are the Secwepemc
    http://secwepemc.sd73.bc.ca
Unoccupied village sites from Teit (1909): "The Shuswap"

Castlegar

## St. Joseph's Residential School

Residential schools in Canada were a partnership between church missionary groups and the federal government. The government funded and regulated the schools while church missionaries operated them.

Residential schools were a major component of the Canadian government's efforts to assimilate Aboriginal people into the dominant white society. The goal was to force Aboriginal people to abandon their culture, spirituality, languages, ethical values, and traditional government and blend into the dominant white society. If successful, assimilation would have removed the government's legal and financial obligations to Aboriginal people as a group and given the colonists control of Aboriginal lands and resources.

The goal of the missionaries was to replace Aboriginal beliefs and practices with Christianity, European moral values, and a settled agricultural life. The missionaries pursued their work with fervor and little financial compensation because they considered it a sacred Christian duty. Both the churches and the government believed that Euro-Canadian culture was superior to that of the Aboriginal people, whom they considered "childlike" and unable to make proper decisions for themselves or their children.

Government and church groups both concluded, after other approaches failed, that assimilation could only be accomplished by isolating Aboriginal children from the influence of their parents at a young age and subjecting them to a rigorous European-style education for several years. The Canadian residential school system was established to accomplish this, and the first schools were built in 1883. Attendance was voluntary at first but the Indian Act was revised in 1894 to make attendance mandatory for all or most of the year. Non-attendance was punishable by parental fines or imprisonment.

St Joseph's Mission was started in 1867 by the Oblates of Mary Immaculate, a French Catholic missionary order who purchased land near Williams Lake, British Columbia. The location was selected partly because of its proximity to three Nations: Secwépemc (Shuswap), Tsilhqot'in (Chilcotin) and Dakelh (Carrier). After acquiring additional land by pre-emption and purchase, the Mission became a productive ranching operation, a base for missionary visits to surrounding Aboriginal communities, and the location of a day school for white and mixed race children.

The Mission day school struggled financially and, in 1891, it was replaced by a residential school for Aboriginal children only. The school was supported by an annual federal grant, but funding was a constant issue and often inadequate to support quality education, care of children, or facility maintenance. The school was attended by children from the three nearby Nations as well as from the St'at'imc (Lillooet) Nation. Most students were Secwépemc. Only a few Tsilhqot'in attended prior to the 1930's. In the first year, eleven boys attended but, by 1950, the number was nearly 300.  Prior to 1953, education included half days of instruction, primarily to prepare boys for agricultural work and girls for domestic work, and half days of industrial labour, with proceeds used to support the school financially. Year-round attendance was required in order for the Oblates to receive their full government grant. The curriculum was designed to prepare students only for low-paying manual labour and did not meet the academic standards of schools for white children.

Teaching methods at the Mission required unquestioning obedience, strict discipline and speaking only in English. Transgressions resulted in harsh punishment.  Hunger was common, food often poor, and sickness rampant in the poorly constructed buildings. The school attempted to destroy students' pride in their heritage, their family and themselves.  The students suffered abuse of all kinds. The student death rate was high, and some who died were not returned to their parents. Dull uniforms were issued to prevent children from having pride in their clothing. Teaching methods and living conditions contrasted sharply with children's home experiences, and many students ran away.

In 1945, the school was declared an extreme fire risk and, in 1952, the dormitory for boys burned to the ground just after a new classroom building had been constructed. In 1964, the school was completely taken over by the Department of Indian Affairs, with the Oblates assuming new roles as counselors rather than teachers. By the mid 1970s, students were living at the residential school, but most were bussed to public schools. The residential school closed in 1981, and the facility was used briefly as Tribal Council offices and an adult training centre. Although the Secwépemc tried desperately to acquire the old school lands owned by the Oblates, the site was sold to a ranch in the late 1980s. The main building was torn down by the ranch over a period of years in the mid to late 1990s.

We would like to acknowledge Ordell Steen, Jean William and Rick Gilbert for their input, which allowed us to present this history to you. Photo Credit- Dave Abbott, St Joseph Mission Circa 1975.

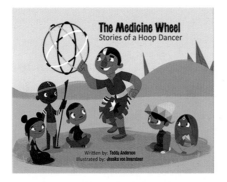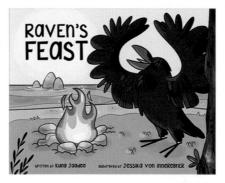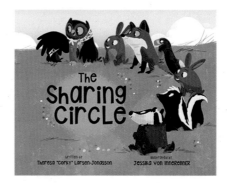
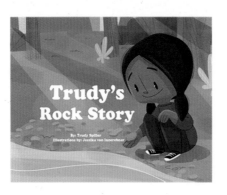

Books for ages 7-12 (available in English and French)

Educational lesson plans and posters
available online!